PRETENDING

PRETENDING

PARUL SINGH NOOR

A Thing Called Love

Love. A word so small, yet it encompasses the vastness of human experience, transcending time, culture, and circumstance. Love is the essence of life, the force that binds us, the emotion that drives us to our greatest heights and our deepest depths. It is both the simplest and the most complex of feelings, capable of bringing immeasurable joy and profound sorrow. Love is a journey, a dance, a story that unfolds in countless ways. This book, "Pretending", is a testament to that journey—an exploration of two souls through poetry navigating the labyrinth of love, from the first spark to the final letting go.

To love is to open oneself to vulnerability. It is to allow another person to see into the deepest recesses of our being, to share our dreams, fears, and insecurities. In the embrace of love, we find a refuge, a sanctuary where we can be our truest selves. Love is the gentle whisper in the night, the comforting presence in moments of doubt, the unspoken understanding that we are not alone. It is the warmth of a hand held, the tenderness of a kiss, a silent support in times of trial.

Love is a paradox. It is strength and weakness, joy and pain, certainty and doubt. To be loved is to be seen and accepted for who we are, with all our imperfections and flaws. It is the assurance that, despite the chaos of the world, there is a place where we belong. Love is the thread that weaves together the fabric of our lives, creating a tapestry of shared moments, memories, and experiences.

In the pages that follow, we delve into the story of two lovers who journey through the many facets of love. From their first glance, where the seeds of affection are planted, to the silent struggles and whispered doubts that test their bond, their story is one of profound connection and inevitable separation. They experience the joy of companionship, the beauty of shared moments, and the bittersweet realization of love. Yet, despite the intensity of their feelings, they ultimately find themselves on separate paths, pretending that all is well, while their hearts tell a different tale.

To understand love is to embrace its contradictions. Love is free, yet it binds us. It is a source of immense joy, yet it can bring unimaginable pain. It is an ever-evolving journey, where the destination is never quite clear, but the experience is what truly matters. In "Pretending," we witness the beauty and tragedy of love, the moments of happiness and the shadows of heartbreak. Through the eyes of our protagonists, we come to appreciate the complexity of love and the courage it takes to truly let go.

Love is not just a feeling; it is an action, a choice, a commitment. It is the willingness to give of oneself without expecting anything in return, to support and uplift, to cherish and protect. Love is the foundation upon which we build our lives, the light that guides us through the darkest of times. It is the reason we strive, the motivation behind our greatest endeavors, and the comfort that sustains us when all else fails.

As you journey through this book, may you find reflections of your own experiences with love. May you be reminded of the beauty of connection, the importance of vulnerability, and the strength that comes from embracing love in all its forms. "Pretending" is more than a poetic story; it is a celebration of love, a recognition of its power, and an acknowledgment of the resilience of the human heart.

In the end, love is what makes us human. It is the essence of our existence, the force that drives us to connect, to create, and to care. It is the thing that makes life worth living, the reason behind our smiles and the solace in our tears.

This book is a tribute to that most wondrous of things—love. May it inspire you to love deeply, to embrace the journey, and to cherish the moments, for it is in love that we find our truest selves.

As you hold this book in your hands, I want to take a moment to share with you the heart and soul that went into creating "Pretending." This story is not just a tale of two lovers, but a reflection of the many faces of love that we encounter throughout our lives. It is an exploration of the intricate dance between heart and mind, the delicate balance of joy and sorrow, and the enduring power of connection. Love is a universal experience, yet it is deeply personal and unique to each individual. It can lift us to the highest peaks and plunge us into the deepest valleys. It can be as fleeting as a whisper or as enduring as the stars. In "Pretending," I sought to capture the essence of this powerful emotion through the journey of two souls whose paths intertwine and diverge, leaving an indelible mark on each other's lives.

The journey of love that unfolds within these pages is inspired by the myriad experiences we all share. It is a tapestry woven from moments of joy and heartache, connection and separation, hope and despair. As you read, you may find echoes of your own experiences, moments that resonate with the love you have known and the pain you have felt. It is my hope that this story will offer you both solace and inspiration, reminding you of the beauty and complexity of love.

Writing this book has been a deeply personal endeavor. It required me to delve into the depths of my own emotions, to confront the vulnerability and strength that love demands. It is a reflection of my belief that love, in all its forms, is worth celebrating and understanding. Whether it is the initial spark of attraction, the deep bond of companionship, or the bittersweet act of letting go, each aspect of love teaches us something profound about ourselves and the world around us. 'Pretending' speaks to the masks we wear, the emotions we hide, and the truths we struggle to face. It is about the delicate balance between what we show the world and what we keep hidden in our hearts.

As you read this book, I hope you will find reflections of your own experiences with love. Whether you are in the throes of a new romance, navigating the complexities of a long-term relationship, or healing from a past heartbreak, I hope this story resonates with you. Love is a universal language, and it is my hope that "Pretending" speaks to your heart and soul.

Lastly, I want to remind you that love, in all its forms, is a beautiful and powerful force. It is the essence of our humanity, the reason behind our smiles and tears, and the light that guides us through the darkest times. Embrace love, cherish the moments, and never be afraid to open your heart.

Mohabbat
Parul Singh Noor

First Light

The First Glance

In summer's glow, on stairs they met
Smiles locked in a silent duet
A poem exchanged, hearts set alight
Love bloomed from that first glance's light
In hallways crossed, a secret dance
A tale of love, born from chance

In summer's golden, gentle light
Two souls converged, by fate's invite

The stairs, a stage for eyes to meet
Where heartbeats quickened, bittersweet

Through hallways long, they'd passed each day
In silent scripts, with much to say

But on these steps, in sudden pause
A spark ignited, without cause

No thoughts of love had crossed their minds
Just daily moments, undefined

Yet here, where sun and shadows blend
A deeper tale began to bend

One offered words in verse, a gift
A poem that made their spirits lift

Lines of longing, love's embrace
Reflected in a lover's grace

The other, touched by each fine phrase
Adored the poet's secret praise

In every line, a truth revealed
A silent pact, their hearts concealed

Eyes locked in tender, soft surprise
A universe within their eyes

No words were spoken, none required
For in that glance, they both conspired

To love, to cherish, yet to wait
To ponder if this was their fate

In summer's warmth, on steps so rare
A love began, beyond compare

Each day henceforth, the hallways knew
Two hearts that beat as one, anew

For in the stairway's brief romance
Was born a love from just one glance

The Whispers

In silent smiles, a language blooms
Unspoken words, like whispered tunes
Each glance, each touch, a silent vow
In silent steps, love finds its how
A dance of hearts, in quiet grace
Unspoken love, in their embrace

In the quiet spaces between their smiles
Unspoken words lingered, mile by mile

With each glance exchanged, a silent vow
Unveiling secrets they held, here and now

They smiled, a language only they knew
In eyes that sparkled, love shining through

Care woven in the threads of their gaze
A tapestry of affection, in silent ways

Excuses found to cross paths each day
In hallways where their hearts would stray

Conversations sparked, brief and light
Yet heavy with the weight of what might

Unspoken words hung in the air
Like petals falling, soft and fair

Each gesture, each touch, a whispered plea
To bridge the chasm between what could be

In stolen moments, their souls would dance
In the silent symphony of chance

But lips remained sealed, hearts dared not speak
For fear of shattering this fragile mystique

Yet in the silence, a love did grow
A tender seed, destined to sow

In the garden of their unspoken dreams
Where reality and fantasy gleams

For sometimes love speaks loudest in the quiet
In the moments when words dare not riot

In the language of touch, of glance, of care
Their unspoken words, a love affair

So let them linger, these words unsaid
In the spaces where their hearts are led

For in the silence, love finds its voice
In the beauty of their silent choice

Intertwining

Embrace

In the warmth of shared moments
Daily talks, in love's gentle light
Their bond deepens, in joy and woe
Companionship's embrace, a gentle flow
Together they walk, hand in hand
In the symphony of love, they stand

In the gentle embrace of companion glow
Two find solace, in each other's flow

With every passing day, they draw near
Sharing hopes and fears, without a fear

Spending hours together, in silent bliss
Talking, laughing, in love's sweet kiss

Their bond grows stronger, day by day
In the warmth of friendships' gentle sway

They speak of dreams, of hopes, of fears
And wipe away each other's tears

No secrets held, no walls to hide
In the sanctuary of love, they confide

Every word exchanged, a precious gift
In the tapestry of love, their spirits lift

They share their joys, their sorrows too
In the comfort of knowing, their love is true

With every sunrise, and every night
They find solace in each other's light

Companions on this journey, hand in hand
Together they'll weather, life's shifting sand

Through valleys low, and mountains high
Their love will guide them, as they fly

For in the sanctuary of companionship's art
They find the whispers of each other's heart

So let them cherish, this bond so rare
In the symphony of love, beyond compare

For in the depths of each other's soul
They find the truest form of whole

Shared Moments

In shared moments, hearts intertwine
Dancing, singing, under stars they shine
Discovering beauty in art and sound
Exploring the world, love knows no bound
In silence, they find solace, hand in hand
A symphony of love, in each shared stand

In the dance of shared moments, hearts entwine
Two souls, in harmony divine

They sway to the rhythm of love's sweet song
 In each other's arms, where they belong

Dancing together under beautiful skies
Their laughter echoes, as time flies

Singing melodies of joy and delight
In harmonies pure, their spirits take flight

Introducing new music, art, and more
Exploring passions, they hadn't explored before

In each brushstroke, in every chord
Their connection deepens, as they're adored

Venturing to places, both near and far
Hand in hand, beneath the evening star

Witnessing wonders, both big and small
In the embrace of love's eternal call

Yet sometimes, in silence, they find their peace
In quiet moments, where all worries cease

Sitting together, no need for words
In the serenity of shared worlds

In these shared moments, a symphony plays
A melody of love that forever stays

For in the tapestry of memories spun
Their bond grows stronger, two hearts as one

Realization

Midnight Confessions

Confessions whispered, hearts entwined
Love's realization, beautifully defined
In tender words, their truth unfurls
A bond of love, in endless swirls
Hand in hand, they embrace the light
In love's realization, pure and bright

Countless confessions whispered in the night
Yet hesitant steps, no one took in sight

Feelings bloomed, like flowers in spring
But fear and doubt kept love's song from singing

Each declaration echoed, heartfelt and pure
Yet silence lingered, a barrier unsure

Until one day, in a moment's grace
They found the courage to embrace

"I love you," they whispered, hearts aglow
A river of emotion, beginning to flow

In each other's eyes, they saw the truth
Love's gentle whisper, undeniable proof

No longer bound by fear's tight hold
In love's embrace, their hearts unfold

They basked in the warmth of affection's light
Knowing now their love was right

Hand in hand, they walked the path
Unfurling love's sweet aftermath

With every step, their bond grew strong
In the realization of love, where they belong

Their journey, though fraught with fear
Led them to love, crystal clear

For in the depths of uncertainty's tide
They found love, steadfast, and tried

The Touch

Love's touch, a language of its own
In tender caress, their hearts are shown
Fingers entwined, they find their way
In each embrace, their love holds sway
With every kiss, their souls ignite
In love's touch, they find delight

In the tender touch of love's embrace
For finding solace, in a sacred space

Fingers intertwined, hearts beat as one
In the language of touch, something begun

A brush of fingertips, a gentle caress
Sends shivers down the spine, a sweet finesse

In each other's arms, they find their rest
As love's soft touch, their spirits blessed

Hands tracing patterns on skin so fair
Speaking volumes in gestures rare

In the warmth of each other's embrace
They find comfort, in love's grace

In moments stolen, in passion's flame
Their bodies merge, without shame

The touch of love, an intimate dance
A symphony of desire, in each glance

With every kiss, with every sigh
Their love deepens, soaring high

For in the touch of love, they find
A connection eternal, intertwined

The Hidden and Shown Letters

In letters hidden, her love blooms
The muse, in verses, she consumes
Each word a tribute, to her grace
In every line, her presence trace
Through poetry's lens, her beauty shines
In hidden letters, love entwines

In the quiet corners of mind
Finding her essence, undefined

In hidden thoughts and whispered sighs
Her presence lingered, a sweet surprise

Each letter penned with tender care
Her image woven, beyond compare

With every word, her beauty shown
In verses crafted, love was known

She, the muse, the guiding light
Inspiring poetry, day and night

In hidden corners of soul
Her essence danced, a love untold

With every stroke of the pen
Her spirit soared, time and again

In verses painted, with hues divine
Her love, her muse, forever entwined

Through sonnets sung and ballads weaved
Her presence lingered, never deceived

In every line, her essence found
In hidden letters, love was crowned

Inner Conflicts

Silent Struggles

Silent struggles bind their hearts tight
Unspoken love in the quiet night
In shared glances, hopes reside
Fear and longing side by side
Hearts confined, yet eyes reveal
A love that waits, yearning to heal

In the quiet corners of their hearts
Silent struggles tear them apart

Unspoken fears, like shadows cast
Haunt their thoughts, a lingering past

He ponders deeply, in sleepless nights
His heart's desire, kept out of sight

In every glance, a question lies
Will one ever dare to break the ties?

She, too, battles within her mind
A storm of feelings, hard to find

Her love a secret, kept so tight
Hidden from the world, in the dark of night

Their smiles, a mask, a careful play
Hiding the words they wish to say

Each touch, a spark, a fleeting chance
Yet fear holds firm, halts their advance

In every shared, silent embrace
Lies a story, full of grace

Unseen wars, within them wage
On the silent struggles stage

They walk together, side by side
With hearts so full, yet worlds divide

A chasm wide, of doubt and fear
Keeps their whispered feelings near

One dreams of moments, brave and bold
Where love's sweet story might be told

But every time, the courage fades
Lost in the silence, love's charades

She writes her love in hidden lines
In secret journals, love confines

Her heart a book, no one can see
Locked away, without a key

In silent struggles, love remains
Bound by fear, by unseen chains

Yet hope still flickers, in their eyes
A love that waits, that never dies

In the quiet, they both long
For a moment, love's true song

To break the silence, free their hearts
And end the struggles, new life starts

Crossroads

At crossroads, hearts ponder fate
Fears and hopes, a silent debate
To speak their love or let it hide
Risking all or safe inside
In choices made, love's truth they'll find
Courage to free, hearts intertwined

At the crossroads of their hearts they stand
Two souls entwined, yet hesitant hands

Questions swirl in their minds each night
Is this love real, is it right?

She wonders if confessing love
Will bring them closer, or push and shove

Will she return the feelings she hides
Or will she turn, let distance divide?

She ponders if her heart should speak
Or if silence means she's weak

Will she see her love as true
Or will revealing tear them in two?

They walk the paths of "if" and "when"
Of love unspoken, again and again

Each step a gamble, each word a risk
In this dance of love, so complex and brisk

Is holding back the safer way
To keep the bond they share each day?

Or does the truth set hearts on fire
And lift their love, higher and higher?

She thinks of moments, smiles shared
Of secrets held, of how they cared

In her heart, a longing grows
But fear and doubt keep doors closed

She dreams of futures bright and warm
Yet shadows whisper, fear the storm

What if love confessed turns to pain
And all they've built washes away in rain?

They stand at crossroads, lost in thought
Each wondering what the other's sought

In silent rooms, they weigh their hearts
Fearing both the ends and the starts

Yet love remains, a guiding star
Pulling them close, though fears bar

In the crossroads of their hearts' deep core
They seek the strength to ask for more

For in the dance of right and wrong
In the heart's most fragile song

The answers lie in steps they take
In courage found, and risks they make

At the crossroads, love's truth awaits
In choices made and opened gates

Together they must choose the way
To speak their love, or let silence stay

Whispers of Doubt

In whispers of doubt, hearts hesitate
Is this true love or merely fate?
Uncertain, they search for a sign
In every touch, in eyes that shine
Yet hope endures through shadowed fears
Seeking truth beyond the tears

In the quiet corners of the night
Whispers of doubt take their flight

Uncertain hearts, caught in between
Wondering what their love might mean

She lies awake, thoughts swirling fast
Is this love real, will it last?

Her heart, a captive, fear's embrace
Questions linger, filling space

She, too, ponders in the dark
Is this true love, a lasting spark?

Or just a dream, a fleeting flame
A moment's passion, without name?

They share their days, their smiles, their fears
Yet doubt persists, it never clears

In every touch, a question lies
Is this the truth, or just disguise?

Whispers of doubt, a constant hum
What if love's end should ever come?

Will they regret the path they take
Or find in love, a sweet escape?

She wonders if her heart is true
If she feels the same way too

Or is she lost in her own mind
A love that's real, or undefined?

She questions if her love will stay
Or fade like night into the day

Is she the one she truly needs
Or just a chapter in her deeds?

Their hearts are full, yet minds confused
In love's embrace, they feel bemused

The whispers linger, soft and low
 Is this the love they wish to know?

In silence shared, they seek a sign
A beacon bright, a love divine

Yet doubt's voice echoes in their ears
A shadowed path, a trail of tears

But in the end, they must decide
To trust in love, or let it slide

For whispers of doubt will always call
But love's true voice can conquer all

In every look, in every touch
They feel the weight, they feel the clutch

Of love unproven, doubt's cruel art
Yet hope remains within their hearts

TURNING POINT

Almost

In the twilight of almost's grasp
Hearts yearn, yet fear holds fast
A touch, a glance, words near spoke
Love's promise in silence broke
At the turning point, they stand
Will they leap or hold love's hand?

In the twilight of their story's arc
Lingers a moment, both bright and dark

An "almost" love, a step not taken
In the silence, hearts awaken

They walked a path, so close, so near
With every glance, a hidden tear

Words unsaid, emotions tight,
In the shadowed dance of night

One reached for another, then drew away
A touch, a breath, both wished to stay

Yet fear held fast, a chain unbroken
In the space between, words unspoken

She felt the pull, the tender sway
In every almost, love's sweet array

Her heart ached for a step ahead
But doubt and caution filled her instead

Moments shared, where time stood still
A lingering glance, a silent thrill

Almost confessed, almost revealed
Love's true depth, almost sealed

In crowded rooms, their eyes would meet
A silent promise, bittersweet

Hands brushed close, yet never held
A story waiting, love compelled

They laughed, they cried, they almost spoke
In every gesture, love's soft cloak

But almost kept them in its thrall
An endless dance, a silent call

One day beneath the blue sky
One almost whispered, "You and I"

One almost answered, "Yes, my dear"
But words dissolved, consumed by fear

In dreams, they find what almost was
A love unfettered, without cause

In waking hours, the truth remains
An almost love, in silent chains

Yet in their hearts, a flicker burns
A hope that someday, love returns

To break the chains of almost's grip
And let their hearts and souls equip

For almost love, though sweetly sung
Is not enough, where hearts are strung

They long for more than almost's dance
To take a step, to seize the chance

At the turning point, they stand once more
Two hearts yearning, forevermore

Will they leap or will they stay
In almost's realm, or love's full sway?

Missed Chances

In the dance of fate, chances slip away
Regrets linger in the shadows of yesterday
Each missed moment, a silent plea
For courage to seize love's decree
Yet hope persists, amidst the pain
In the belief that love will find its reign

In the tapestry of their intertwined fate
Lies the threads of chances, tempting, yet late

Moments slipped by, like grains of sand
Leaving behind regrets, heavy and grand

They walked parallel paths, so close, yet apart
Each chance encounter, a missed start

In crowded rooms, their eyes would meet
But words remained unspoken, a silent defeat

Opportunities danced in the moonlit night
But hesitation kept their love from taking flight

A touch, a smile, a fleeting glance
All lost in the shadows of circumstance

They danced around their feelings, afraid to confess
Each missed chance a dagger in their hearts' distress

Regrets whispered in the silence of the night
As they wondered what could have been, if they'd taken
flight

In the quiet of their thoughts, they replayed the scenes
Each missed chance haunting, like half-forgotten
dreams

They longed to rewind time, to seize the day
To bridge the gap between what they feel and what they
say

But time marched on, and chances slipped away
Leaving behind the ache of what they didn't say

They watched as others found love's sweet embrace
While they remained trapped in their own heart's maze

Yet amidst the pain of missed chances and regrets
A glimmer of hope lingered, refusing to forget

For even in the darkest night, stars still shine bright
And perhaps, in the future, love will finally take flight

So they hold onto hope, despite the missed chances past
Believing that true love will find them at last

For in the tapestry of fate, there's always a thread,
A chance for love to bloom, despite what's left unsaid.

The Distance

In silence, they stand, worlds apart
The distance grows, an ache in the heart
Reasons many, yet none at all
Society's whispers, pride's cruel call
Timings off, flaws laid bare
Love's silent plea, lost in despair

A chasm wide, a silent divide
Between two hearts, once side by side

No words exchanged, no reasons why
Just silence lingering, beneath the sky

The distance grows, a quiet ache
As they drift apart, with each mistake

Society's whispers, right and wrong
Echo in their minds, a lingering song

Timings off, and flaws revealed
Insecurities shielded, emotions concealed

They yearn to bridge the gap, to cross the line
But fear holds them back, frozen in time

Misunderstandings breed in the silence
Fueling the flames of their defiance

What once was love, now feels unsure
Lost in the depths of doubt obscure

They long to reach out, to break the spell
But pride and ego keep them in their shell

So they watch from afar, with hearts in pain
As the distance widens, like a growing stain

Each passing day, the gap expands
As they struggle to grasp love's gentle hands

But the distance remains, a silent wall
As they stand on opposite sides, alone in the fall

Yet amidst the silence, a flicker of hope
That someday, somehow, they'll learn to cope

 For love knows no bounds, no distance too far
And in the end, it's love that heals the scar

Acceptance

Looking Back

In reflections, they find love's grace
Moments cherished, in time and space
Laughter echoes, memories bright
In the embrace of love's sweet light
Accepting fate's twists, they find peace
In looking back, love's story won't cease

In the quiet of solitude, they pause to reflect
On the tapestry of moments, love did perfect

Each memory a gem, polished with care
In the gallery of their hearts, treasures rare

They recall the laughter, the smiles so bright
In the warmth of love's embrace, shining light

Hand in hand, they walked the path of dreams
Through valleys low and sun-kissed streams

They remember the whispers, the secrets shared
In the safety of love's sanctuary, bared

Their souls intertwined, in a dance divine
A symphony of love, forever entwined

In the echoes of laughter, they find solace sweet
In the embrace of memories, they feel complete

For though their journey took unexpected turns
In each other's arms, their love still burns

They accept the twists of fate, the roads they've trod
Knowing that love transcends the whims of God

For in looking back, they see love's true art
A masterpiece painted on the canvas of their heart

So they cherish the moments, both joyous and sad
For each one a testament, to the love they had

And though they may part, and go their separate ways
Their love remains eternal, a beacon that stays

The Broken Hearts

In silence, they bear the weight of shattered dreams
Two broken hearts, adrift in silent streams
Yet in their pain, they find release
Embracing the brokenness, seeking peace
Through tears and ache, they walk the path
Knowing healing lies beyond love's aftermath

In the shattered silence of their parting
Two broken hearts, quietly departing

No words exchanged, no tears to shed
Just emptiness lingering, in shades of red

Each beat a reminder of love's demise
A symphony of sorrow, beneath the skies

They walk alone, yet side by side
In the shadows of love, they both reside

Pain echoes in the chambers of their souls
Like shattered glass, beyond control

They ache in silence, with every breath
In the aftermath of love's untimely death

They hold the pieces of their shattered dreams
In trembling hands, where hope now gleams

Yet in the brokenness, they find release
Embracing the pain, seeking inner peace

For though their hearts are rent in two
They find strength in what they once knew

In the quiet acceptance of love's decay
They find solace in the light of day

They walk the path of healing, slow but sure
In the depths of pain, they find the cure

For broken hearts may ache and mourn
But from the ashes, new hope is born

So they embrace the brokenness, the pain
Knowing that healing will come again

For in the shattered pieces of their hearts
They find the courage for new starts

What Ifs and Maybes

In the realm of "what ifs," dreams take flight
In the land of "maybes," hope ignites
Imagining a world where love's at hand
Holding onto possibilities, grand
But in the end, reality's stark
Yet in "maybes," they find a spark

In the realm of "what ifs" they dwell
Where fantasies bloom and stories swell

Imagining a world where they're together
In love's embrace, hearts lighter than a feather

What if they hadn't been torn apart
By the whims of fate, a cruel heart?

Would they stroll hand in hand, beneath the stars
Free from the burden of love's scars?

What if their laughter echoed loud and clear
In a world where love conquers fear?

Would they dance in the rain, without a care
Knowing their love is strong, beyond compare?

What if they whispered secrets in the night
 In the soft glow of love's gentle light?

Would they share dreams, hopes, and fears
As they journey through the passing years?

What if they kissed beneath the moon's soft glow
In a love that's timeless, ebb and flow?

Would they find solace in each other's arms
Safe from the world's ever-present harms?

What if they gazed into each other's eyes
And saw the truth, with no disguise?

Would they know that love's sweet embrace
Is worth every risk, every chase?

But in the end, the "what ifs" fade away
As reality dawns with the light of day

For though they dream of what could be
They accept the truth of what they see

So they cherish the moments, however brief
And hold onto hope, beyond belief

For in the realm of "what ifs" they find
The power to keep love's flame alive

In the land of "maybes," they reside
Where dreams take flight, and hearts decide

Perhaps in another time, another place
They'd find love's warmth, in each other's embrace

Maybe fate had different plans in store
Guiding them apart, forevermore

But in the whispers of "maybes," they find
A glimmer of hope, in the depths of their mind

Maybe they missed their chance to shine
To intertwine their hearts, to call each other mine

But in the maybes' dance, they hold onto
The possibility of a love that's true

Maybe they'll meet again someday
In a twist of fate, a serendipitous way

And in that moment, they'll finally see
That "maybes" can turn to certainty

Maybe love's flame will never die
Despite the tears, the heartache, the sigh

For in the "maybes" lies a spark
A chance for love to leave its mark

Maybe they'll look back and understand
Why things unfolded the way they planned

And in the end, they'll realize
That "maybes" led them to their prize

But until then, they'll hold onto hope
In the land of "maybes," they'll learn to cope

For in every "maybe," there's a chance
To find love's sweet, enduring dance

So they'll embrace the uncertainty
And trust in the power of destiny

For in the realm of "maybes," they'll find
That love's journey is one of a kind

The Closure

Letting Go

In the quiet of farewell, they stand
Love's gentle grip, released by hand
Tears shed for what they cannot keep
 In letting go, love's whispers sleep
Hearts heavy with the weight of goodbye
But in release, they find love's sky

In the quiet of their parting, they stand
Two souls intertwined, hand in hand

Love still lingers, in the space between
But they know it's time to set love free

With heavy hearts, they say goodbye
Tears glistening, beneath the sky

Each word a struggle, each moment a pain
As they release the love they can't contain

They hold onto memories, cherished and dear
But know it's time to let go, to steer

Their separate ways, in search of peace
In the bittersweet release.

For love remains, a gentle flame
But sometimes letting go is love's true aim

In the silence of their parting, they find
The courage to leave love behind

They walk away, with hearts still sore
But know they'll heal, and hurt no more

For in letting go, they find release
In the embrace of love's sweet peace

So they bid farewell, with love in their eyes
Knowing that sometimes, love means goodbye

For in the letting go, they find the key
To set their hearts and spirits free

Love is Free, Freedom is Love

Love's essence, pure and true
In freedom's embrace, it blooms anew
For love is freedom, and freedom, love
In open skies, they rise above
Bound by love's bond, yet free to soar
In freedom's dance, they find amore

In the dance of love, they find their way
Embracing freedom, in love's sway

For love knows no bounds, no chains to bind
It thrives in freedom's gentle wind

In letting go, they set love free
A truth as clear as the deep blue sea

For love is not possession, nor control
It's the freedom to fly, heart and soul

They understand that love's true essence
Lies in the beauty of its independence

It's the choice to stay, the choice to roam
To build a life together, or to walk alone

In love's embrace, they find release
In the freedom to be, to love, to cease

For love is not a cage, nor a tether
It's the open sky, in all its weather

They cherish each other, yet give space
Knowing that love's beauty lies in grace

 In the freedom to grow, to change, to evolve
They discover that love is freedom's resolve

So they walk hand in hand, yet walk apart
Bound by love's bond, but free in heart

For love is free, and freedom is love
A truth as pure as the stars above

Moving On

In love's journey, they found new shores
Embracing the past, as it no longer roars
With open hearts, they now move on
To new beginnings, where love is drawn
Memories cherished, but futures bright
In moving on, they find love's light

In the tapestry of life, they found new threads
Weaving love anew in different beds

Their hearts, once intertwined, now apart
Embracing the journey, a brand new start

They bid farewell to what once was
With gratitude for love's sweet applause

For though their paths diverged, they know
Love's beauty remains, in the ebb and flow

With open hearts, they embrace the new
Giving their all to love that's true

In the arms of another, they find solace sweet
As they embark on love's joyful beat

They carry the memories, cherished and dear
But know it's time to let go of fear

For in moving on, they find release
In the promise of a love that won't cease

They cherish the lessons learned along the way
And hold onto hope for a brighter day

For though they've loved and lost before
They know that love opens new doors

So they embrace the present, with hearts aglow
Knowing that love's journey continues to grow

In moving on, they find love's sweet song
As they dance to the rhythm, forever strong

PRETENDING

In hallways bright with summer's glow
Two souls passed, yet didn't know

 A glance, a spark, no intention clear
Just two hearts, quietly near

A poem exchanged, love's first light
In verses soft, hearts took flight

Smiles began, care slowly grew
In corridors where secrets flew

Unspoken words, silent glances
Love's dance in subtle trances

Excuses made, to meet and share
In whispered words, beyond compare

Companionship bloomed, day by day
In shared moments, hearts found their way

Talking, laughing, joys and tears
Together facing, hopes and fears

Realization dawned, love confessed
Countless feelings, hearts expressed

Yet no steps taken, love held tight
In the shadows, fear and light

Touches tender, love's embrace
In each other, found their place

Yet society's chains, right and wrong
Held them back, love's silent song

In hidden letters, love's muse seen
Poetry flowed, hearts serene

Yet silent struggles, doubts arose
In love's shadow, fears opposed

At crossroads, hearts questioned deep
Right or wrong, love's secrets keep

Whispers of doubt, silent and still
Is this love, or fate's cruel will?

Almost reached, yet held at bay
Love's turning point, twilight gray

Missed chances, linger in mind
Regret and hope, intertwined

The distance grew, hearts apart
Silent reasons, broke their heart

In letting go, love's gentle release
Finding strength, in silent peace

What ifs and maybes, dreams and schemes
In love's realm, where hope redeems

In moving on, new love they found
Yet memories linger, love's sweet sound

Pretending now, all is fine
Love's past, a distant line

They smile and laugh, masks in place
Hiding the heartache, no trace

In public eyes, they're strong and free
Yet love's ghost whispers, silently

Pretending strength, hiding the pain
Love's essence, a lingering stain

They walk apart, paths diverged
In their hearts, love's song submerged

Pretending all is well, they stride
With love's truth, hidden inside

For though they act, as if unscathed
 Love's deep wounds, cannot be swayed

Pretending happiness, smiles bright
In the quiet, love's lost light

In the end, love's journey shown
Happy and sad, they've grown

Pretending peace, they move along
Yet in their hearts, love's lasting song

In the dance of life, they play their part
Pretending ease, with heavy hearts

They meet and chat about the day
Like old friends in a casual way

They're talking small, like "how you been?
How's your mom? How's life been?"

They laugh at jokes, share trending news
Ignoring the past, avoiding clues

One cracks a joke about a kiss
She laughs it off, avoiding bliss

As if the thought doesn't cause her pain
As if she's not longing to feel again

They pretend it's simple, that they're okay
Masking the hurt, pushing it away

As if that person's not what she's waiting for
As if she's not the one she's longing for

For now, they both keep pretending
Hiding the truth, their hearts defending

She waves goodbye, she drives away
Each aching for the words they can't say

The window down, their eyes still meet
She says goodnight, her heart's discreet

Wishing she'd turn back, never leave
Typing texts she'll never conceive

"You're everything," she wants to say
But silence keeps her thoughts at bay

For now, they both keep on pretending
Each heart in silence, slowly mending

They walk away, their paths diverge
But in their minds, old feelings surge

In crowded rooms, they hide their ache
Smiling through the pain they fake

Pretending joy in every scene
While memories haunt where they have been

They cherish moments, yet hide the pain
Replaying love's sweet, tender refrain

In dreams, they hold what they let go
But waking brings the truth they know

The dance of love, now bittersweet
In silence, their hearts still beat

Pretending they're just friends, it's fine
Ignoring the love they left behind

Each touch remembered, each word unsaid
In the silence, love is fed

For now, they'll both keep pretending
Hiding the wounds that need mending

In the quiet of the night, they lie
Thinking of each other with a sigh

As if they're not what they're waiting for
As if love's not knocking at their door

For now, they both keep pretending
Hoping time will bring an ending

But until then, they wear their masks
Hiding love in mundane tasks

Pretending they're okay, they smile
Knowing truth lies in the trial

For now, they keep on pretending
In hopes of a love unending

A Thing Called Love

A thing called love, so pure and true
A light that shines in all we do

It lifts us up, it brings us down
In its embrace, we laugh, we drown

In love's first glance, a spark ignites
A dance of hearts beneath the lights

With tender touch and whispered words
Two souls unite like flocks of birds

It starts with smiles and gentle care
With fleeting glances, moments rare

In every touch, a story told
A silent bond begins to hold

Companionship, a growing flame
Two lives entwined, never the same

They share their days, their nights, their dreams
In love's soft glow, a steady beams

Through ups and downs, through joy and pain
Love's gentle hand, a constant reign

Unspoken words, yet understood
In silent struggles, they've withstood

At crossroads faced, with hearts so torn
They ponder love, both night and morn

Is this the path that's meant to be?
In love's deep sea, they search for free

Whispers of doubt, yet love remains
In every joy, in all the pains

Two hearts in sync, yet often strained
In love's embrace, they are sustained

Almost there, yet just out of reach
Love's lesson, life continues to teach

Missed chances haunt, yet hope endures
For love's sweet promise still allures

The distance grows, they drift apart
Yet love's soft echo fills the heart

Pretending all is well, they smile
While memories linger, mile by mile

Looking back, the moments shared
In love's warm light, their souls laid bare

The joy, the pain, the highs, the lows,
In love's great tapestry, it shows

Broken hearts and silent tears
Yet love remains through all the years

They move beyond, find new embraces
Yet love's sweet ghost in empty spaces

A thing called love, both strong and fragile
A journey long, a path so agile

In every heart, it leaves its mark
A flame that lights the deepest dark

Love is free, and freedom's love
A soaring spirit, a gentle dove

In letting go, they find their peace
In love's release, their hearts increase

For love is more than what they've known
In every seed that love has sown

It grows and blooms, it fades and dies
Yet always lives in lovers' eyes

Through all the joy and all the strife
Love is the essence of our life

A thing called love, forever new
In every heart, it beats so true.

Missed chances haunt, yet hope endures
For love's sweet promise still allures

The distance grows, they drift apart
Yet love's soft echo fills the heart

Pretending all is well, they smile
While memories linger, mile by mile

Looking back, the moments shared
In love's warm light, their souls laid bare

The joy, the pain, the highs, the lows,
In love's great tapestry, it shows